WITH OPEN HANDS

Other books by
HENRI J. M. NOUWEN
published by Ave Maria Press

Behold The Beauty of the Lord
Out of Solitude
In Memoriam
Heart Speaks to Heart

WITH OPEN HANDS

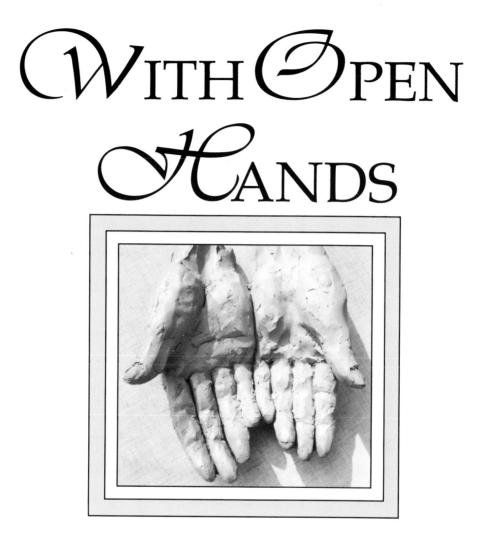

HENRI J. M. NOUWEN

PHOTOGRAPHY

Jean-Claude Lejeune, George R. Merrill and Marie Antoinette Parisio

AVE MARIA PRESS
NOTRE DAME, INDIANA 46556

International Standard Book Number: 0-87793-545-9

Library of Congress Catalog Card Number: 94-79358

Cover and text design by Katherine Robinson Coleman

"Open Hands" cover sculpture by Suzanne M. Young

Photography:

Jean-Claude Lejeune 10, 17, 22, 25, 29, 36, 42, 47, 50, 55, 64, 69, 72, 76, 79, 87, 88, 98.

George R. Merrill 13, 27, 28, 33, 39, 45, 46, 56, 60, 68, 90, 101, 105, 107, 114, 116, 118, 120-121, 123, 128.

Marie Antoinette Parisio 6, 12, 19 , 20, 32, 34, 35, 38, 44, 52, 62, 65, 70, 73, 81, 84, 85, 90, 96, 99, 103, 110, 111, 118, 126, 129, 130, 131.

Ron van den Bosch 16, 133.

Printed and bound in the United States of America.

CONTENTS

Preface

The ideas gathered together in this book were slow in coming. They originated in an attempt to speak personally about a number of experiences with prayer. I felt that I should not write about prayer without having asked the question: "What is it that I myself find in prayer?" I came to see that praying had something to do with silence, with acceptance, with hope, with compassion, and even with criticism. Then I carefully sought out concepts and images which expressed what I had experienced or would have liked to experience.

But aren't my own experiences so personal that they might just as well remain hidden? Or could it be that what is most personal for me, what rings true in the depths of my own being, also has meaning for others? Ultimately, I believe that what is most personal is most universal. To arrive at this point, however, friends are necessary to help distinguish superficial, private sensations from deep, personal experiences.

This conviction led me to invite twenty-five theology students to form a group which would start with my own hesitant formulations and help develop a common understanding of what is truly involved in prayer. We held seven meetings, during which there was little discussion or argumentation, but much sharing of lived experiences. Gradually, the elusive phenomenon we call prayer became a tangible reality.

The following reflections, therefore, are not the work of a single author. They were born during many hours of intimate and prayerful conversation. I hope that they will bear fruit not only in the lives of those who took part in these conversations, but also in the lives of the readers who will spend a few quiet moments with this book.

Utrecht, 1971

Nearly twenty-five years after writing this preface, I can say that my hope that the words on prayer written in this book would bear fruit in people's lives, has been fulfilled in ways that I never could have predicted. Countless men and women from the most different ages, cultures and religions have told me in spoken or written words that the movement from clenched fists to open hands, described in this book, has helped them to understand the meaning of prayer and has in fact helped them to pray. I am deeply grateful for these responses, especially since they affirm the mysterious truth that something universal can be found in the most intimate center of our hearts. When we—twenty-five students and myself—sat around a classroom table in 1970 in a small town in the Netherlands, none of us could have foreseen the fruits of our spiritual conversations. I have no idea where these students are today, but I know now what I didn't know then, that the Spirit of God was among us and allowed us to be an instrument of grace.

Since this book was first published, much has happened in church and society, but the challenge to enter into the presence of God with open hands is still there, more urgent than ever. When I think about my own struggle with prayer I realize that these reflections written more than two decades ago, are calling me today, as never before, to a radical conversion of mind and heart. And once again I hope that this will be true for many others as well.

Toronto, 1994

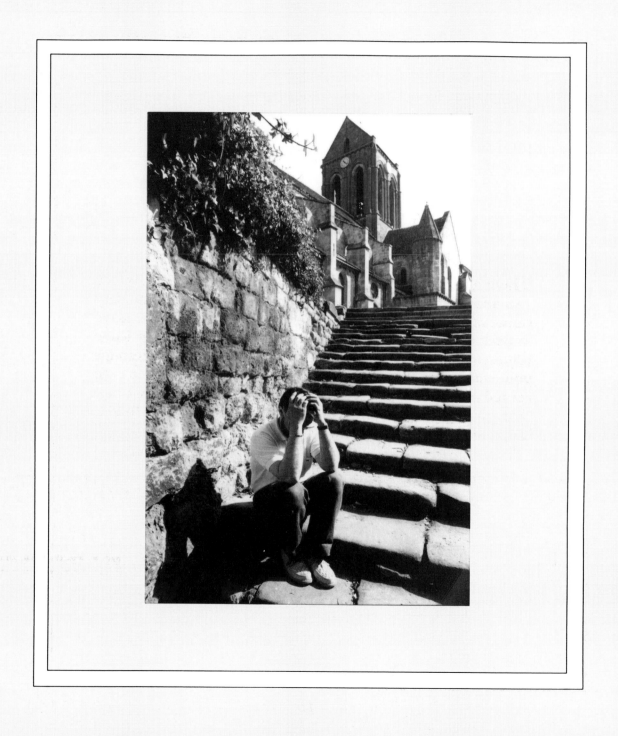

Introduction

With clenched fists

Praying is no easy matter. It demands a relationship in which you allow someone other than yourself to enter into the very center of your person, to see there what you would rather leave in darkness, and to touch there what you would rather leave untouched. Why would you really want to do that? Perhaps you would let the other cross your inner threshold to see something or to touch something, but to allow the other into that place where your most intimate life is shaped—that is dangerous and calls for defense.

The resistance to praying is like the resistance of tightly clenched fists. This image shows a tension, a desire to cling tightly to yourself, a greediness which betrays fear. A story about an elderly woman brought to a psychiatric center exemplifies this attitude. She was wild, swinging at everything in sight, and frightening everyone so much that the doctors had to take everything away from her. But there was one small coin which she gripped in her fist and would not give up. In fact, it took two people to pry open that clenched hand. It was as though she would lose her very self along with the coin. If they deprived her of that last possession, she would have nothing more and be nothing more. That was her fear.

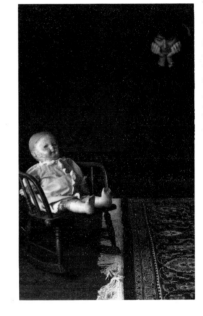

*W*hen you are invited to pray, you are asked to open your tightly clenched fists and give up your last coin. But who wants to do that? A first prayer, therefore, is often a painful prayer because you discover you don't want to let go. You hold fast to what is familiar, even if you aren't proud of it. You find yourself saying: "That's just how it is with me. I would like it to be different, but it can't be now. That's just the way it is, and this is the way I'll have to leave it." Once you talk like that you've already given up believing that your life might be otherwise. You've already let the hope for a new life float by. Since you wouldn't dare to put a question mark after a bit of your own experience with all its attachments, you have wrapped yourself up in the destiny of facts. You feel it safer to cling to a sorry past than to trust in a new future. So you fill your hands with small, clammy coins which you don't want to surrender.

You still feel bitter because people weren't grateful for something you gave them, you still feel jealous of those who are better paid than you are, you still want to take revenge on someone who didn't respect you, you are still disappointed that you've received no letter, still angry because someone didn't smile when you walked by. You live through it, you live along with it as though it didn't really bother you…until the moment when you want to pray. Then everything returns: the bitterness, the hate, the jealousy, the disappointment and the desire for revenge. But these feelings are not just there; you clutch them in your hands as if they were treasures you didn't want to let go. You sit wallowing in all that old sourness as if you couldn't do without it, as if, in giving it up, you would lose your very self.

Detachment is often understood as letting loose of what is attractive. But it sometimes also requires letting go of what is repulsive. You can indeed become attached to dark forces such as resentment and hatred. As long as you seek retaliation, you cling to your own past. Sometimes it seems as though you might lose yourself along with your revenge and hate—so you stand there with balled-up fists, closed to the other who wants to heal.

*W*hen you want to pray, then, the first question is: How do I open my closed hands? Certainly not by violence. Nor by a forced decision. Perhaps you can find your way to prayer by carefully listening to the words the angel spoke to Zechariah, Mary, the shepherds, and the women at the tomb: "Don't be afraid." Don't be afraid of the One who wants to enter your most intimate space and invite you to let go of what you are clinging to so anxiously. Don't be afraid to show the clammy coin which will buy so little anyway. Don't be afraid to offer your hate, bitterness and disappointment to the One who is love and only love. Even if you know you have little to show, don't be afraid to let it be seen.

*O*ften you will catch yourself wanting to receive your loving God by putting on a semblance of beauty, by holding back everything dirty and spoiled, by clearing just a little path that looks proper. But that is a fearful response — forced and artificial. Such a response exhausts you and turns your prayer into torment.

*E*ach time you dare to let go and to surrender one of those many fears, your hand opens a little and your palms spread out in a gesture of receiving. You must be patient, of course, very patient until your hands are completely open.

*I*t is a long spiritual journey of trust, for behind each fist another one is hiding, and sometimes the process seems endless. Much has happened in your life to make all those fists, and at any hour of the day or night you might find yourself clenching your fists again out of fear.

*M*aybe someone will say to you, "You have to forgive yourself." But that isn't possible. What is possible is to open your hands without fear, so that the One who loves you can blow your sins away. Then the coins you considered indispensable for your life prove to be little more than light dust which a soft breeze will whirl away, leaving only a grin or a chuckle behind. Then you feel a bit of new freedom, and praying becomes a joy, a spontaneous reaction to the world and the people around you. Praying then becomes effortless, inspired and lively, or peaceful and quiet. When you recognize the festive and the still moments as moments of prayer, then you gradually realize that to pray is to live.

Dear God,

I am so afraid to open my clenched fists!
Who will I be when I have nothing left to hold on to?
Who will I be when I stand before you with empty hands?
Please help me to gradually open my hands
and to discover that I am not what I own,
but what you want to give me.
And what you want to give me is love,
unconditional, everlasting love.

Amen.

Question for meditation:

What am I holding tightly in my clenched fist?

One

*P*RAYER AND SILENCE

*W*e know there is some connection between prayer and silence, but if we think about silence in our lives, it seems that it isn't always peaceful, silence can also be frightening.

*O*ne student who had thought deeply about the silence in his life wrote:

Silence is night
and just as there are nights
with no moon and no stars
when you're all alone
totally alone
when you're cursed
when you become a nothing
which no one needs—
so too there are silences
which are threatening
because there is nothing except the silence.
Even if you open your ears
and your eyes
it keeps going on
without hope or relief.
Night with no light, no hope
I am alone
in my guilt
without forgiveness
without love.
Then, desperately, I go looking for friends
then I walk the streets searching for a body
a sign
a sound
finding nothing.

But there are also nights
with stars
with a full moon
with the light from a house in the distance
and silences which are peaceful and reflective
the noise of a sparrow
in a large empty church
when my heart wants to sing out with joy
when I feel that I'm not alone
when I'm expecting friends
or remember a couple words
from a poem I read lately
when I lose myself in a Hail Mary
or the somber voice of a psalm when I am me
and you are you
when we aren't afraid of each other
when we leave all talk to the angel
who brought us the silence
and peace.

*J*ust as there are two nights, there are two silences: one is frightening, the other peaceful. For many, silence is threatening. They don't know what to do with it. If they leave the noise of the city behind and come upon a place where no cars are roaring by, no ships tooting, no trains rumbling; where there is no hum of radio or television, where no CDs or tapes are playing, they feel their entire bodies gripped by an intense unrest. They feel like a fish thrown on dry land. They have lost their bearings. Some people can't study without a solid wall of music surrounding them. If they are forced to sit in a room without a constant flow of sound, they grow very nervous.

Thus, for many of us, silence has become a threat. There was a time when silence was normal, and a lot of noise disturbed us. But today, noise is the normal fare, and silence—strange as it may seem—has become the disturbance. It is not hard to understand that people who experience silence in this way have difficulty with prayer.

We have become alienated from silence. If we go to the beach or on a picnic in the woods, the walkman is often our most important companion. It seems that we can't bear the sound of silence.

Silence is full of sounds: the wind murmuring, the leaves rustling, the birds flapping their wings, the waves washing ashore. And even if these sounds cannot be heard, we still hear our own quiet breathing, the motion of our hands over our skin, the swallowing in our throats and the soft patter of our footsteps. But we have become deaf to these sounds of silence.

When we are invited to move from our noisy world into this sound-filled silence, we often become frightened. We feel like children who see the walls of a house collapse and suddenly find themselves in an open field, or we feel as though we have been violently stripped of our clothing, or like birds torn away from their nests. Our ears begin to ache because the familiar noise is missing; and our bodies have become used to that noise as if it were a downy blanket keeping us warm. We become like addicts who must go through the painful process of withdrawal.

*B*ut still more difficult than getting rid of these exterior noises is the achievement of inner silence, a silence of the heart. It seems that a person who is caught up in all that noise has lost touch with the inner self. The questions which are asked from within remain unanswered. Unsure feelings are not cleared up; tangled desires are not straightened out, and confusing emotions are not understood. All that remains is a chaotic tumble of feelings which have never had a chance to be sorted out.

It is hardly surprising, then, that when we shut off all the daily racket, a new inner noise can often be heard, rising from all those chaotic feelings screaming for attention. Entering into a quiet room doesn't automatically bring us inner silence. When there is no one to talk to or to listen to, an interior discussion may start up—often noisier than the noise we just escaped. Many unsolved problems demand attention; one care forces itself upon the other; one complaint rivals the next; all pleading for a hearing. Sometimes we are left powerless in the face of the many twisted sentiments we cannot untangle.

*I*t makes you wonder if the diversion we look for in the many things outside us might not be an attempt to avoid a confrontation with what is inside. "What should I do when I'm through with all my work?" This question leads many people to flee from themselves and hold fast to any number of things which make them feel as if they're still busy. It's as if they were saying: "Where do I turn when I have no more friends to talk with, no music to listen to, no paper to read and no films to see?" The question is not whether we can live without friends or without feeding our eyes and ears with new impressions—we obviously cannot—but whether we can stand to be alone from time to time, shut our eyes, gently push aside all the assorted noises and sit calmly and quietly.

To be calm and quiet by yourself is not the same as sleeping. In fact, it means being fully awake and following with close attention every move going on inside you. It requires the discipline to recognize the urge to get up and go again as a temptation to look elsewhere for what is close at hand. It offers the freedom to stroll in your own inner yard and rake up the leaves and clear the paths so you can easily find the way to your heart. Perhaps there will be fear and uncertainty when you first come upon this "unfamiliar terrain," but slowly and surely you will discover an order and a familiarity which deepens your longing to stay at home.

*W*ith this new confidence, we recapture our own life afresh, from within. Along with the new knowledge of our "inner space" where feelings of love and hate, tenderness and pain, forgiveness and greed are separated, strengthened or reformed, there emerges the mastery of the gentle hand. This is the hand of the gardener who carefully makes space for a new plant to grow and who doesn't pull weeds too rashly, but uproots only those which threaten to choke the young life.

*U*nder this gentle regime, we can once again become masters in our own house. Not only during the day, but during the night as well. Not only when we are awake, but also when we sleep. For the one who has the day, will gain the night as well. Sleep is no longer a strange darkness, but a friendly curtain behind which dreams continue to speak and to send out messages which can be gratefully received. The paths of our dreams become as trustworthy as the paths of our waking hours and there is no longer any need to be afraid.

*I*f we do not shun silence, all this becomes possible — but not easy. Noise from the outside keeps demanding our attention, and restlessness from within keeps stirring up our anxiety. Many people feel trapped between this temptation and this fear. Since they can't turn inward, they look for calm in the noises, even when they know they will never find it there.

*B*ut whenever you do come upon this silence, it seems as though you have received a gift, one which is "promising" in the true sense of the word. The promise of this silence is that new life can be born. It is this silence which is the silence of peace and prayer because it brings you back to the One who is leading you. In this silence you lose the feeling of being driven, and you find that you are a person who can be yourself along with other people.

Then you realize that you can do many things, not compulsively but freely. It is the silence of the "poor in spirit," where you learn to see your life in its proper perspective. In this silence, the false pretenses fade away, and you can see the world again with a certain distance, and in the midst of all your cares, you can pray:

Dear God,

Speak gently in my silence.
When the loud outer noises of my surroundings
and the loud inner noises of my fears
keep pulling me away from you,
help me to trust that you are still there
even when I am unable to hear you.
Give me ears to listen to your small, soft voice saying:
"Come to me, you who are overburdened,
and I will give you rest…
for I am gentle and humble of heart."
Let that loving voice be my guide.

Amen.

Question for meditation:

Why do I avoid silence?

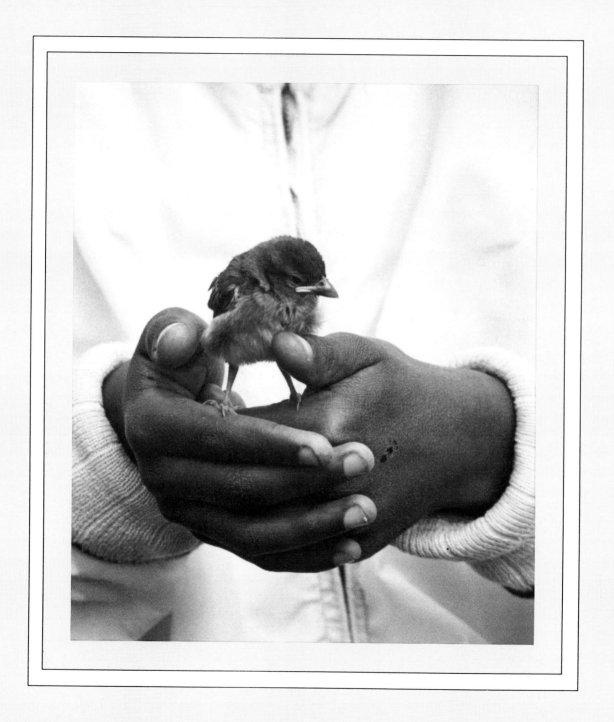

Two

PRAYER AND ACCEPTANCE

Deep silence leads us to realize that prayer is, above all, acceptance. When we pray we are standing with our hands open to the world. We know that God will become known to us in nature around us, in people we meet, in situations we run into. We trust that the world holds God's secret within it, and we expect that secret to be shown to us. Prayer creates that openness in which God is given to us. Indeed, God wants to be admitted into the human heart, received with open hands, and loved with the same love with which we have been created.

This openness, however, does not come simply of itself. It requires a confession that you are limited, dependent, weak and even sinful. Whenever you pray, you profess that you are not God nor do you want to be God, that you haven't reached your goal yet, that you never will reach it in this life, that you must constantly stretch out your hands and wait for the gift of life. This attitude is difficult because it makes you vulnerable.

The wisdom of the world is the wisdom which says: "It is best to stand firm, to get a good grip on what's yours here and now and hold your own against the rest who want to take it away from you; you've got to be on your guard against ambush. If you don't carry a weapon, if you don't make a fist and don't scramble to get what little you need—food and shelter—then you're just asking to be threadbare and destitute, and you'll end up trying to find a mediocre satisfaction in a generosity which no one appreciates. You open your hands and they pound in nails! Smart people keep on their toes, with muscles tense and fists clenched; they squint and are always ready for an unexpected attack."

That's how a person's inner life often appears. If you nurture thoughts of peace, you have to be open and receiving. But can you do it, do you dare? Suspicion, jealousy, hate, revenge, resentment and greed are there before you've even given them a name. "What are they really trying to do?" "What's actually on their minds?" "They must not be laying all their cards on the table." "There's certainly more to that remark than meets the eye." Often such feelings arise even before thoughts can be formulated. Something deep inside has already tightened up: "Watch out, plan your tactics and hold your weapons in readiness." And so thoughts of peace remain far away. You fear they are too dangerous or impractical. You think: "Those who don't arm themselves share the guilt for their own fall."

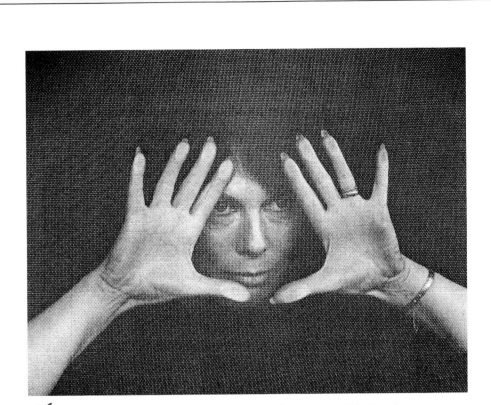

How can you expect a gift in such a mood? Can you even imagine that your life could be any other way? No wonder praying presents such a problem, for it requires a constant readiness to lay down your weapons and let go of feelings which tell you to keep a safe distance. It requires you to live in the constant expectation that God, who makes everything new, will cause you to be born again.

You become a person only when you are capable of standing open to all the gifts which are prepared for you.

Giving can easily become a means of manipulation where the one who receives a gift becomes dependent on the will of the one who gives it.

When you give, you are the master of the situation, you can dole out the goods to those you think deserving. You have control over your milieu, and you can enjoy the power your possessions give you.

*A*cceptance is something else. When we accept a gift, we invite others into our world and are ready to give them a place in our own lives. If we give gifts to our friends, we expect them to give them a place in their home. Ultimately, gifts become gifts only when they are accepted. When gifts are accepted, they acquire a place in the life of the receiver. It is understandable that many people want to give a gift in return as soon as possible, thereby reestablishing the balance and getting rid of any dependent relationship. We often see more trading than accepting. Many of us are even embarrassed with a present because we know not how to reciprocate. "It makes me feel obligated," we often say.

$\mathcal{P}$erhaps the challenge of the gospel lies precisely in the invitation to accept a gift for which we can give nothing in return. For the gift is the life breath of God, the Spirit poured out on us through Jesus Christ. This life breath frees us from fear and gives us new room to live. Those who live prayerfully are constantly ready to receive the breath of God and to let their lives be renewed and expanded. Those who never pray, on the contrary, are like children with asthma: because they are short of breath, the whole world shrivels up before them. They creep into a corner gasping for air and are virtually in agony. But those who pray open themselves to God and can breathe freely again. They stand upright, stretch out their hands and come out of their corner, free to move about without fear.

When we live from God's breath we can recognize with joy that the same breath that keeps us alive is also the source of life for our brothers and sisters. This realization makes our fear of the other disappear, our weapons fall away and brings a smile to our lips. When we recognize the breath of God in others we can let them enter our life and receive the gifts they offer us.

The difficulty this presents in our time comes out in this not so unusual confession: "To accept something gives me a feeling of dependence. This is something I'm generally not used to. I manage my own affairs and I'm glad I can. Whenever I receive something, I don't know exactly how to handle it. It's as though I am no longer in control of my own life and it gets a little uncomfortable. Actually, that's a silly thing to say, for I'm not letting others have what I myself like to have...I don't let them have the joy of giving."

But when we notice that someone really accepts us fully, we want to give everything we can and often discover in the giving that we have much more than we thought.

In this prayerful acceptance of each other, there is no place left for prejudice because instead of defining others, we let them appear to us as ever new. Then we can speak to each other and share our lives in such a way that heart speaks to heart. One student writes: "A good conversation is a process where we give each other the strength to go on, to celebrate together, to be sad together and to inspire one another."

*P*raying means, above all, to be accepting toward God who is always new, always different. For God is a deeply moved God whose heart is greater than ours. The open acceptance of prayer in the face of an ever-new God makes us free. In prayer, we are constantly on the way, on a pilgrimage. On our way, we meet more and more people who show us something about the God whom we seek. We will never know for sure if we have reached God. But we do know that God will always be new and that there is no reason to fear.

*P*rayer gives us the courage to stretch out our arms and to be led. After Jesus had given Peter the commission to care for his people, he said:

> *I* tell you most solemnly,
> when you were young
> you put on your own belt
> and walked where you liked;
> but when you grow old
> you will stretch out your hands,
> and somebody else will put a
>   belt around you
> and take you where you would
>   rather not go—John 21:18.

To care for others requires an ever-increasing acceptance. This acceptance led Jesus and his disciples to where they did not want to go—to the cross. That is also the road of those who pray. When you are still young, you want to hold everything in your own hands, but when you have grown older and opened your hands in prayer, you are able to let yourself be led without knowing where. You know only that the freedom which God's breath has brought you will lead to new life, even if the cross is the only sign you can see.

But for the one who prays, even that sign will have lost its fearful character.

Dear God,

I so much want to be in control.
I want to be the master of my own destiny.
Still I know that you are saying:
"Let me take you by the hand and lead you.
Accept my love
and trust that where I will bring you,
the deepest desires of your heart will be fulfilled."
Lord open my hands to receive your gift of love.

Amen.

Question for meditation:

In what ways am I afraid of dependence?

Three

PRAYER AND HOPE

In the silence of prayer you can spread out your hands to embrace nature, God and your fellow human beings. This acceptance means not only that you are ready to look at your own limitations, but that you expect the coming of something new. For this reason, every prayer is an expression of hope. If you expect nothing from the future, you cannot pray. Then you say with Bertold Brecht:

As it is, it will stay

What we want will never come.

If you think this way, life stands still. Spiritually, you are dead. There can be life and movement only when you no longer accept things as they are now and look ahead toward that which is not yet.

However, when it comes to prayer, it seems that we do more asking than hoping. This is not surprising, since we pray mostly when very specific and often momentary circumstances ask for it. When there is war, we pray for peace; when there is drought, we pray for rain; when we go on vacation, we pray for nice weather; when a test is coming, we pray that we'll pass; when friends are sick, we pray that they will get well; and when they die, we pray for their eternal rest. Our prayer emerges in the midst of our lives and is interwoven with everything else which busies our day. Whatever fills the heart is what the mouth pours forth. This is also true of prayer.

Our hearts are filled with many concrete, tangible desires and expectations. A mother hopes her son will come home on time. A father hopes he'll get a promotion. A boy dreams of the girl he loves, and the child thinks of the bicycle she was promised. Often our thoughts are no further than a couple of hours, a couple of days, a couple of weeks ahead of us, seldom as much as a couple of years. We can scarcely let ourselves think too far in advance, for the world we live in requires us to focus our attention on the here and now. If we pray, and really pray, we can hardly escape the fact that our cares for the moment, big and small, will fill our prayer and often make it nothing but a long list of requests.

*O*ften this prayer of petition is treated with a certain disdain. Sometimes we regard it as less noble than prayer of thanksgiving and certainly less noble than prayer of praise. Prayer of petition is supposedly more egocentric because we are putting our own interests first and trying to get something for ourselves. The prayer of thanksgiving, it is said, is directed more toward God, even if it is in connection with gifts that God has given us. The prayer of praise is supposedly directed completely to God, independently of anything we may or may not have received.

*B*ut the question is whether this distinction helps us understand what prayer is. The important thing about prayer is not whether it is classified as petition, thanksgiving or praise, but whether it is a prayer of hope or of little faith.

The prayer of little faith makes us cling to the concrete circumstances of the present situation in order to win a certain security. The prayer of little faith is filled with wishes which beg for immediate fulfillment. This kind of prayer has a Santa Claus naiveté about it and wants the direct satisfaction of very specific wishes and desires. When this prayer is not heard, that is, when we don't get the presents we wanted, there is disappointment, even hard feelings and bitterness.

It is understandable, therefore, that this prayer of little faith carries a great deal of fear and anxiety with it. If you pray with little faith for health, success and advancement, for peace or whatever else, then you get so set on the concrete request that you feel left out in the cold when the expected answer doesn't come. You even say to yourself: "See what I told you, it doesn't work anyway."

*W*ith this prayer of little faith, it is the concreteness of the wishes which eliminates the possibility for hope. In this prayer, you want to be certain about what is uncertain, and you say to yourself that a bird in the hand is better than two or ten birds still in the bush. With this prayer, your petition is aimed at getting what you ask for, any way you can, instead of being directed toward the person who might or might not make that wish come true. People of little faith pray like children who want a present from Santa Claus but who are so frightened of the "Holy Man" that they run away as soon as they have their hands on their package. They would rather have nothing more to do with the old bearded gentleman than getting his gift. All the attention is on the gift and none on the one who gives it. When we pray this way, our spiritual life is reduced to a beeline toward what we want.

*B*eing so eager to arrange our own future, we of little faith close ourselves off from what is coming. We have no patience with the unspecified promises and we have no trust in the unseen situations which the future has in store. Therefore, when we pray with little faith, we pray without hope. Likewise, we pray without despair, for despair is possible only for someone who knows what it means to hope.

The prayer of little faith is carefully reckoned, even stingy, and is upset by every risk. There is no danger of despair and no chance for hope. We become midgets in a world of tiny things.

The immense difference between hope and wishfulness comes out in the remarks of a student who wrote: "I see hope as an attitude where everything stays open before me. Not that I don't think of my future in those moments, but I think of it in an entirely different way. Daring to stay open to whatever will come to me today, tomorrow, two months from now or a year from now—that is hope. To go fearlessly into things without knowing how they'll turn out, to keep on going, even when something doesn't work the first time, to have trust in whatever you're doing—that is living with hope."

*W*hen we live with hope we do not get tangled up with concerns for how our wishes will be fulfilled. So, too, our prayers are not directed toward the gift, but toward the one who gives it. Our prayers might still contain just as many desires, but ultimately it is not a question of having a wish come true but of expressing an unlimited faith in the giver of all good things. You wish that...but you hope in...

In the prayer of hope, there are no guarantees asked, no conditions posed and no proofs demanded. You expect everything from the other without binding the other in any way. Hope is based on the premise that the other gives only what is good. Hope includes an openness by which you wait for the promise to come through, even though you never know when, where or how this might happen.

*P*erhaps, in the long run, there is no finer image for the prayer of hope than the trusting relation of little children toward their mother. All day long they ask for things, but the love they have for their mother does not depend on her fulfilling all these wishes. Little children know that their mother will do only what is good for them, and in spite of occasional fits and a few short-lived tantrums if they don't get their way, they continue to be convinced that, in the end, their mother does only what she knows is best for them.

When you pray with hope you may still ask for many concrete things; like nice weather or a better salary. This concreteness can even be a sign of authenticity. For if you ask only for faith, hope, love, freedom, happiness, modesty, humility, etc., without making them concrete in the nitty-gritty of daily life, you probably haven't involved God in your real life. If you pray in hope, all those concrete requests are ways of expressing your unlimited trust in God who fulfills all promises, who holds out for you nothing but good and who wants to share goodness and love with you.

Only if you pray with hope can you break through the barriers of death. For no longer do you want to know what it will be like after you die, what heaven will look like exactly or how you will be eternal. You don't let yourself be distracted by daydreams in which all your conflicting desires are satisfied in a wish-come-true hereafter. When you pray with hope, you turn yourself toward God, trusting fully that God is faithful and makes all promises real.

This hope gives you a new freedom which allows you to look realistically at life without feeling dejected. This freedom comes through in the words of another student who wrote:

*H*ope means to keep living
amid desperation
and to keep humming
in the darkness.
Hoping is knowing that there is love,
it is trust in tomorrow
it is falling asleep
and waking again
when the sun rises.
In the midst of a gale at sea,
it is to discover land.
In the eyes of another
it is to see that you are understood....

*A*s long as there is still hope
There will also be prayer....

*A*nd you will be held
in God's hands.

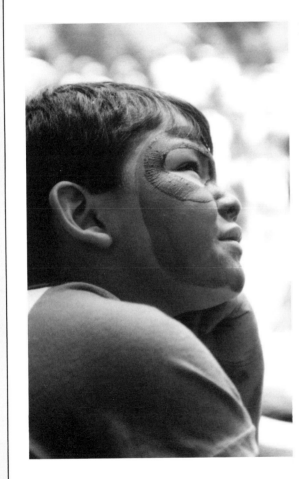

Thus, every prayer of petition becomes a prayer of thanksgiving and praise as well, precisely because it is a prayer of hope. In the hopeful prayer of petition, we thank God for God's promise and we praise God for God's faithfulness.

Our numerous requests simply become the concrete way of saying that we trust in the fullness of God's goodness. Whenever we pray with hope, we put our lives in the hands of God. Fear and anxiety fade away, and everything we are given and everything we are deprived of is nothing but a finger pointing out the direction of God's hidden promise which one day we shall taste in full.

Dear God,

I am full of wishes,
full of desires,
full of expectations.
Some of them may be realized, many may not, but in the
   midst of all my satisfactions and disappointments,
I hope in you.
I know that you will never leave me alone
and will fulfill your divine promises.
Even when it seems that things are not going my way,
I know that they are going your way
and that in the end your way is the best way for me.
O Lord, strengthen my hope,
especially when my many wishes are not fulfilled.
Let me never forget that your name is Love.

Amen.

Question for meditation:

Can my hope in God grow deeper and stronger even when
my many wishes remain unfulfilled?

Four

PRAYER AND COMPASSION

If you are to have a future, it will be a future together with others. A prayer of hope is a prayer that disarms you and extends you far beyond the limits of your own longings. Therefore, there can be no talk of prayer so long as praying is thought of as an activity which excludes our neighbor. "Anyone who says, 'I love God,' and hates his brother or sister is a liar," says St. John (1 John 4:20). And Jesus says: "It is not those who say to me, 'Lord, Lord,' who will enter the kingdom of heaven, but those who do the will of my Father in heaven" (Matthew 7:21).

*Pr*aying can never be antisocial or asocial. Whenever we pray and leave out our neighbors, our prayer is not real prayer. True prayer by its nature is socially significant. But that is not as simple as it sounds. Often people say: "Go out and do something for those who suffer instead of praying for them." Although there is little reason to suppose that so little is done for people who suffer because so much time is spent praying for them, there is some reason to wonder whether the comment "I'll pray for you," is a sign of genuine concern.

In the thinking of our modern, active, energetic world, praying and living have come to be so widely separated that bringing them together seems almost impossible. But here lies the central problem: How can our prayer be truly necesary for the welfare of our fellow human beings? What do we mean when we say that we should "pray always" and that prayer is the "one thing necessary"?

The question becomes important only when it is posed in its most radical form. The question of when or how to pray is not really the most important one. The crucial question is whether we should pray always and whether our prayer is necessary. Here, the stakes are all or nothing! If we say that it's good to turn to God in prayer for a spare minute, or if we grant that a person with a problem does well to take refuge in prayer, we have as much as admitted that praying is on the margin of life and doesn't really matter.

If we think that a little praying can't do any harm, we will soon find that it can't do much good either. Prayer has meaning only if it is necessary and indispensable. Prayer is prayer only when we can say that without it, we cannot live. How can this be true, or be made true? The word that brings us closest to an answer to this question is the word "compassion." To understand this, we must first examine what happens to us when we pray. Then we can comprehend how we can meet our neighbors in prayer.

*Of*ten it is said, that prayer is simply an expression of helplessness. It is asking from another what we cannot do ourselves. This is a half-truth. The praying person not only says, "I can't do it, and I don't understand it," but also, "Of myself, I don't have to be able to do it, and of myself, I don't have to understand it." When you stop at that first phrase, you often pray in confusion and despair, but when you can also add the second, you feel your dependence no longer as helplessness but as a happy openness to others.

If you view your weakness as a disgrace, you will come to rely on prayer only in extreme need and come to consider prayer as a forced confession of your impotence. But if you see your weakness as that which makes you worth loving, and if you are always prepared to be surprised at the power the other gives you, you will discover through praying that living means living together.

A prayer that makes you lose heart can hardly be called a prayer. For you will lose heart when you presume that you must be able to do everything yourself, that every gift to you from the other is a proof of your inferiority and that you are a full person only when you no longer have any need of the other.

*B*ut with this mindset you become weary and exhausted from your efforts to prove you can do it alone, and every failure becomes cause for shame. You lose your buoyancy and become bitter. You conclude that other people are enemies and rivals who have outwitted you. Thus you condemn yourself to loneliness because you perceive every hand which reaches out to you as a threat to your sense of honor.

*W*hen God asked Adam, "Where are you?" Adam answered, "I was hiding" (Genesis 3:9-10). He confessed his true condition. This confession opened him to God. When we pray, we come out of our shelters and not only see our own nakedness but also see that there is no enemy to hide from, only a friend who likes nothing better than to clothe us with a new coat. Certainly praying takes some admissions. It requires the humble recognition of our condition as broken human beings. However, prayer does not lead us to shame, guilt, or despair, but rather to the joyful discovery that we are only human and that God is truly God.

*I*f we cling tightly to our own weakness, our faults, shortcomings and our twisted past, to all the events, facts and situations which we would prefer to cut out of our own history, we are only hiding behind a hedge through which everyone can see. What we have done is to narrow our world to a small hiding place where we try to conceal ourselves, suspecting rather pitifully that everyone has seen us all along.

$\mathcal{P}$raying means giving up a false security, no longer looking for arguments which will protect you if you get pushed into a corner, no longer setting your hope on a couple of lighter moments which your life might still offer. To pray means to stop expecting from God the same small-mindedness which you discover in yourself. To pray is to walk in the full light of God and to say simply, without holding back, "I am human and you are God." At that moment, conversion occurs, the restoration of the true relationship. A human being is not someone who once in a while makes a mistake, and God is not someone who now and then forgives. No! Human beings are sinners and God is love. The conversion experience makes this obvious with stunning simplicity and disarming clarity.

This conversion brings with it the relaxation which lets you breathe again and puts you at rest in the embrace of a forgiving God. The experience results in a calm and simple joy. For then you can say: "I don't know the answer, and I can't do this thing, but I don't have to know it, and I don't have to be able to do it." This new knowledge is the liberation which gives you access to everything in creation and leaves you free to play in the garden that lies before you.

*W*hen you pray, you discover not only yourself and God, but also your neighbor. For in prayer, you profess not only that people are people and God is God, but also, that your neighbor is your sister or brother living alongside you. For the same conversion that brings you to the painful ackowledgment of your wounded human nature also brings you to the joyful recognition that you are not alone, but that being human means being together.

*A*t precisely this point, compassion is born. This compassion is not covered by the word "pity," nor by the word "sympathy." Pity connotes too much distance. Sympathy implies an exclusive nearness. Compassion goes beyond distance and exclusiveness.

Compassion grows with the inner recognition that your neighbor shares your humanity with you. This partnership cuts through all walls which might have kept you separate. Across all barriers of land and language, wealth and poverty, knowledge and ignorance, we are one, created from the same dust, subject to the same laws and destined for the same end. With this compassion you can say, "In the face of the oppressed I recognize my own face and in the hands of the oppressor I recognize my own hands.

$\mathcal{T}$heir flesh is my flesh; their blood is my blood; their pain is my pain; their smile is my smile. Their ability to torture is in me, too; their capacity to forgive I find also in myself: There is nothing in me that does not belong to them, too. There is nothing in them that does not belong to me, too. In my heart, I know their yearning for love, and down to my entrails I can feel their cruelty. In another's eyes, I see my plea for forgiveness, and in a hardened frown, I see my refusal. When someone murders, I know that I too could have done that, and when someone gives birth, I know that I am capable of that as well. In the depths of my being, I meet my fellow humans with whom I share love and hate, life and death."

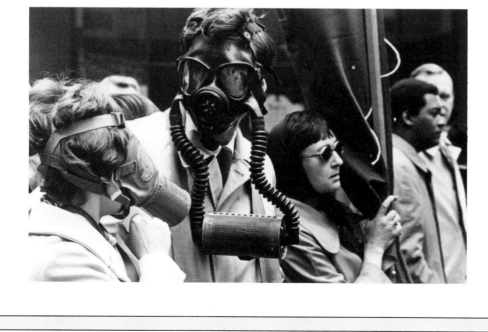

*C*ompassion is daring to acknowledge our mutual destiny so that we might move forward, all together, into the land which God is showing us. Compassion also means sharing in joy, which can be just as important as sharing in pain. To give others the chance to be completely happy, to let their joy blossom to the full. We offer real comfort and support when we can say from our hearts: "That's really good for you," or "I'm glad to see you made it."

$\mathcal{B}$ut this compassion is more than a shared slavery with the same fear and the same sighs of relief and more than a shared joy. For if your compassion is born of prayer, it is born of your meeting with God who is also the God of all people. At the moment that you fully realize that the God who loves you unconditionally loves all your fellow human beings with the same love, a new way of living opens itself to you. For you come to see with new eyes those who live beside you in this world. You realize that they too have no reason to fear, that they too do not have to hide behind a hedge, that they too need no weapons to be human. You see that the inner garden of love which has remained unattended for so long is also meant for them.

Conversion to God, therefore, means a simultaneous conversion to the other persons who live with you on this earth. The farmer, the worker, the student, the prisoner, the sick, the black person, the white person, the weak, the strong, the oppressed and the oppressor, the patient and the one who heals, the tortured and the torturer, not only are they people like you, but they are also called to recognize with you that God is a God for all people.

And so, compassion removes all pretensions, just as it removes false modesty. It invites you to understand everything and everyone, to see yourself and others in the light of God and to joyfully tell everyone you meet that there is no reason to fear; the land is free to be cultivated and to yield a rich harvest.

It is not so simple, however. Risks are involved. For compassion means to build a bridge to others without knowing whether they want to be reached. Your brother or sister might be so embittered that he or she doesn't expect anything from you. Then your compassion stirs up enmity, and it is difficult not to become sour yourself and say, "You see what I told you, it doesn't work anyhow."

And yet, compassion is possible when it has roots in prayer. For in prayer you do not depend on your own strength, nor on the good will of another, but only on your trust in God. That is why prayer makes you free to live a compassionate life even when it does not evoke a grateful response or bring immediate rewards.

Dear God,

As you draw me ever deeper into your heart,
I discover that my companions on the journey
    are women and men
loved by you as fully and as intimately as I am.
In your compassionate heart, there is a place for all of them.
No one is excluded.
Give me a share in your compassion, dear God,
so that your unlimited love may become visible
in the way I love my brothers and sisters.

Amen.

Question for meditation:

How can I recognize the suffering of my sisters and brothers
in my own heart?

Five

PRAYER AND PROPHETIC CRITICISM

As your life becomes more and more a prayer, you not only come to a deeper insight into yourself and your neighbor, but you also develop a better feeling for the pulse of the world you live in. If you are really praying, you can't help but have critical questions about the great problems with which the world is grappling, and you can't avoid the thought that a conversion is not only necessary for yourself and your neighbor, but for the entire human community. The conversion of the world calls for a prophetic witness who dares to criticize the world.

*A*t first glance, the words "prayer" and "criticism" seem to be at such opposite extremes and to come from such different worlds that their combination probably invokes deep frustration. We realize that our world needs to change and that no change will ever happen without action, but often feel lost when it comes to questions of "how"? This frustration is a good place to begin, for in our day, the frustrated person seems to ask for more attention than the person who prays.

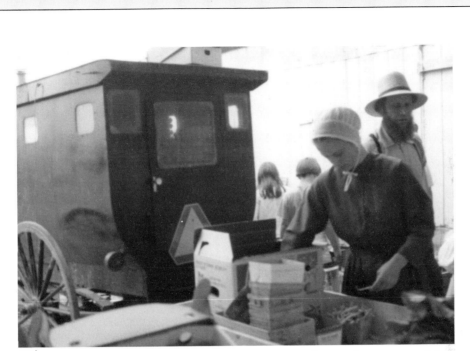

The frustration which gets so many people up in arms, which confuses them and prompts them to protest and demonstrate—or, in defiance, to do nothing or flee into a drugged oblivion—is an unmistakable sign of a deeply-rooted dissatisfaction with the world in which we are forced to live out our lives. Some would like to remind our society of those ideals of freedom and justice which are written in books but which are trampled underfoot in everyday practice. Some have given up this effort and have come to the conclusion that the only chance left for a person to find peace and calm is to retreat from this chaotic world. They turn in disgust from society and its institutions.

*W*hatever one does, whether one becomes a revolutionary or a meek dreamer, whether one calls for the changing of structures or lets it all float by with a melancholy grin, the resentment remains, fierce and discernible or deeply suppressed beneath an attitude of passive indifference. It is not hard to distinguish in all these phenomena a deep longing for another world. Society as it is now must change, its false structures must disappear, and something entirely new must take their place.

*S*ome go into the struggle with all the energy they can muster, while others wait for a new world as for an apparition which they cannot bring about themselves. Still others try to anticipate the future and melt into a forced dreamworld of sound, color and form in which, at least for a moment, they can pretend that everything—even they themselves—has already been transformed.

What is perhaps most striking about today's visions of the world's future is that they have mostly taken shape independently of Christian thinking. The voices which cry out for a new age, a new order, are often heard outside the Christian tradition.

*A*nd yet you are Christian only so long as you look forward to a new world, only so long as you constantly pose critical questions to the society in which you live, and only so long as you emphasize the need for conversion both for yourself and for the world. You are Christian only so long as you, in no way, let yourself become established in a situation of seeming calm, only so long as you stay unsatisfied with the status quo and keep saying that a new world is yet to come. You are Christian only when you believe that you have a role to play in the realization of this new kingdom and when you urge everyone you meet with a holy unrest to make haste so that the promise might soon be fulfilled. So long as you live as a Christian you keep looking for a new order, a new structure, a new life.

*A*s a Christian it is hard to bear with people who stand still along the way, lose heart and seek their happiness in little pleasures which they cling to. It irritates you to see things established and settled, and you feel sad about all that self-indulgence and self-satisfaction, for you know with an indestructible certainty that something greater is coming, and you've already seen the first rays of light. As a Christian, you not only maintain that this world will pass, but that it must pass to allow a new world to be born, and that there will never be a moment in this life when you can rest assured that there is nothing more to do.

*B*ut are there any Christians? If you get the impression that Christianity today is failing in its role of spiritual leadership, if it appears that people seek for the meaning of being and non-being, of birth and death, of loving and being loved, of being young and growing old, of giving and receiving, of hurting and being hurt and expect no response from the witnesses to Jesus Christ, then you begin to wonder to just what degree these witnesses should be calling themselves Christians.

The Christian witness is a critical witness because the Christian professes that the Lord will come again and make all things new. The Christian life calls for radical changes because the Christian assumes a critical distance from the world and, in spite of all contradictions, keeps saying that a new way of being human and a new peace are possible. This critical distance is an essential aspect of true prayer.

*I*t is not so much a question of making a Christian into an activist as of being willing to recognize in the contemporary prophet challenging the "status quo," the authentic features of Christ. For maybe in this person who makes no peace with the world and who is totally dedicated to the struggle for a better future, we can once more find him who gave his life for the freedom of many.

What are the features which mark true prophets? Whenever we look for them, we must understand that these features will never be perfectly evident in any individual person. It is always a question of footprints or notches on a tree which make us suspect that someone has passed by who is worth getting to know.

*W*ho are these revolutionaries? Critical prophets are people who attract others by their inner power. Those who meet them are fascinated by them and want to know more. All who come in contact with them get the irresistible impression that they derive their strength from a hidden source which is strong and rich. An inner freedom flows out from them, giving them an independence which is neither haughty nor aloof, but which enables them to stand above immediate needs and most pressing necessities.

*T*hese critical prophets are moved by what happens around them but don't let it oppress or shatter them. They listen attentively, speak with a self-possessed authority but don't easily get rushed or excited. In everything they say and do, it seems as though there is a lively vision before them which those who hear them can intimate, but not see. This vision guides their lives. They are obedient to it. Through it they know how to distinguish what is important from what is not. Many things which seem of gripping immediacy scarcely stir them, and they attach great importance to some things which others simply let pass.

$\mathcal{A}$s critical Christians, they are not insensitive to what motivates others, but they evaluate what they see and hear around them in the light of their own vision. They are happy and glad to have people listen to them, but are not out to form groups around themselves. No cliques can grow up around them for they attach themselves exclusively to no human being. What they say and do has a convincing ring and even a self-evident truth, but they force their opinions on no one and are not annoyed when someone doesn't adopt their opinion or doesn't do as they wish.

In everything, they seem to have a concrete and living goal in mind, the realization of which is of vital importance. Yet a great inner freedom is maintained in the light of this goal. Often they seem to know that they will never see their goal achieved and that they see only the shadow of it themselves. But, throughout, they have an impressive freedom from the course of their own life. They are careful and cautious, certainly not reckless, and yet it comes out at every turn that they count their own lives as of secondary importance. They don't live to maintain the status quo but to work out a new world, the outlines of which they see and which appeal to them so much that even the fear of death no longer has a decisive power over them.

*B*ut it is also clear that people are repelled as well as drawn to these critical prophets. The offense that is provoked is just as great a reality as the attractiveness displayed. Precisely because they are so free from things which many others hold as unchangeable, they are a threat. Their manner of speaking and living constantly relativizes the values upon which many of us have built our lives. We feel the penetrating depth of the prophetic message and see the consequences for ourselves if we should grant its truth.

*A*gain and again, when these prophets are among us, we know that the reality they live in is also the reality we ourselves are longing for, but which seems to demand too much. In order to uphold our tranquility of mind and no longer be disturbed in our "secure" way of life, we find it necessary to silence those who fight against our artificial happiness.

𝒫ersons, therefore, who proclaim a new world and set the old world reeling, become the occasion for a stifling oppression at the hands of those very ones who consider themselves the protectors of order and the upholders of peace and calm. For those who want to maintain calm and order in the present-day world, these visionaries unmask the illusion of the age and are intolerable agitators. The aggression stirred up against them usually results in their excommunication, with all the means the prevailing order has at its disposal.

*T*his can start with a denial of their message, expand to verbal attacks and end with imprisonment and even execution. But if these critical prophets are credible and true, not even death disrupts their calling. Those who kill them will often discover, to their surprise and horror, that they have only succeeded in awakening many others and that the cry for a new world has grown still louder.

$\mathcal{F}$rom this description, no one in our milieu may qualify as a critical prophet. Names we might mention offer only small traces of the true prophet. And yet it must be said that when we open our eyes and look for visionaries we find them among the thousands whom we meet during our lifetime. Sometimes only vaguely recognizable, sometimes undeniably but never totally evident, they become visible for those who want to see.

We can see the visionary in the guerilla fighter, in the youth with the demonstration sign, in the quiet dreamer in the corner of a cafe, in the soft-spoken monk, in the meek student, in the mother who lets her son go his own way, in the father who reads to his child from a strange book, in the smile of a girl, in the indignation of a worker, in every person who in one way or another draws life from a vision which is seen shining ahead and which surpasses everything ever heard or seen before.

*W*hat does this have to do with prayer? Praying means breaking through the veil of existence and allowing yourself to be led by the vision which has become real to you. Whatever we call that vision: "the Unseen Reality," "the total Other," "the Spirit," "the Father," we repeatedly assert that it is not we ourselves who possess the power to make the new creation come to pass. It is rather a spiritual power which has been given to us and which empowers us to be in the world without being of it.

The praying person looks on the world with compassion, penetrates its hidden meaning and calls it to an always deeper conversion.

Often we use the word God. This word can suggest something fascinating as well as something horrible, attractive as well as repelling, seductive as well as dangerous, all-absorbing as well as nourishing. It is like the sun. Without the sun, there can be no life, but if we come too close to it, we are burned. The Christian, however, believes that God is not "something," but a person who is Love — perfect Love. The Christian knows it is possible to enter into dialogue with this loving God and so work at renewing the earth. Praying, therefore, is the most critical activity we are capable of, for when we pray, we are never satisfied with the world of here and now and are constantly striving to realize the new world, the first glimmers of which we have already seen.

*W*hen you pray, you open yourself to the influence of the Power which has revealed itself as Love. That Power gives you freedom and independence. Once touched by this Power, you are no longer swayed back and forth by the countless opinions, ideas and feelings which flow through you. You have found a center for your life, a center that gives you a creative distance so that everything you see, hear and feel can be tested against the source.

*C*hrist is the one, who in the most revealing way, made clear that prayer means sharing in the power of God. Through this power he turned his world around. He freed countless men and women from the chains of their existence, but also stirred up the aggression which brought him to his death. Christ, who is fully human and fully divine, has shown us what it means to pray. In him, God became visible for the fall and rise of many.

Prayer is a prophetic matter because, once you begin, you put your entire life in the balance. If you really set about praying, that is, truly entering into the reality of the unseen, you must realize that you are daring to express a most fundamental criticism, a criticism which some are waiting for, but which will be too much for many others.

$\mathcal{P}$raying, therefore, means being constantly ready to let go of your certainty and to move beyond where you now are. It demands that you leave your house and take to the road again and again, and always look forward to a new land for yourself and others. This is why praying demands poverty, that is, the readiness to live a life in which you have nothing to lose so that you can always begin afresh. Whenever you willingly choose this poverty you make yourself vulnerable, but you also become free to see the world and to let the world show itself in its true form. You have no need to defend yourself. You can proclaim loudly what you know through your intimate contact with God, who is the source of all life.

*B*ut this demands courage. If you are to make real all the consequences of a prayerful life, you might well get frightened and wonder if you can take the risks. In those times it is vital to remember that courage is also a gift from God for which you can pray with words like these:

Dear God,

Give me the courage to live and work
for a new heaven and a new earth as Jesus did.
Give me the freedom to be critical where I see evil
and to offer praises where I see good.
Most of all, make me faithful to the vision you have
    given me,
so that wherever I go and whomever I meet,
I can be a sign of your all-renewing love.

                  Amen.

Question for meditation:

How can I claim my call to renew the world in the
name of Jesus?

Conclusion

*W*ITH OPEN HANDS

To pray means to open your hands before God. It means slowly relaxing the tension which squeezes your hands together and accepting your existence with an increasing readiness, not as a possession to defend, but as a gift to receive. Above all, prayer is a way of life which allows you to find a stillness in the midst of the world where you open your hands to God's promises and find hope for yourself, your neighbor and your world. In prayer, you encounter God not only in the small voice and the soft breeze, but also in the midst of the turmoil of the world, in the distress and joy of your neighbor and in the loneliness of your own heart.

Prayer leads you to see new paths and to hear new melodies in the air. Prayer is the breath of your life which gives you freedom to go and to stay where you wish and to find the many signs which point out the way to a new land. Praying is not simply some necessary compartment in the daily schedule of a Christian or a source of support in time of need, nor is it restricted to Sunday mornings or mealtimes. Praying is living. It is eating and drinking, action and rest, teaching and learning, playing and working. Praying pervades every aspect of our lives. It is the unceasing recognition that God is wherever we are, always inviting us to come closer and to celebrate the divine gift of being alive.

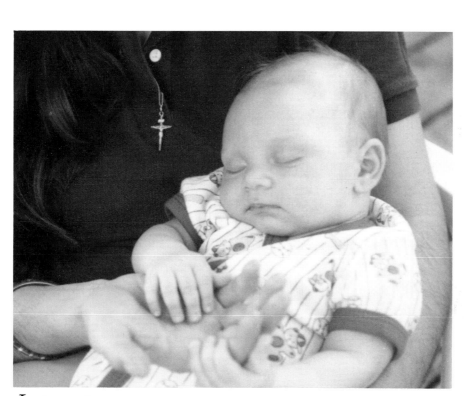

*I*n the end, a life of prayer is a life with open hands where we are not ashamed of our weakness but realize that it is more perfect for us to be led by the Other than to try to hold everything in our own hands.

*O*nly within this kind of life does a spoken prayer make sense. A prayer in church, at table or in school is only a witness to what we want to make of our entire lives. Such a prayer reminds us that praying is living and it invites us to make this an ever-greater reality. Thus, there are as many ways to pray as there are moments in life. Sometimes we seek out a quiet spot and want to be alone, sometimes we look for a friend and want to be together. Sometimes we like a book, sometimes we prefer music. Sometimes we want to sing out with hundreds, sometimes only whisper with a few. Sometimes we want to say it with words, sometimes with a deep silence.

*I*n all these moments, we gradually make our lives more of a prayer and we open our hands to be led by God even to places we would rather not go.

Dear God,

I do not know where you are leading me.
I do not even know what my next day,
my next week or my next year will look like.
As I try to keep my hands open,
I trust that you will put your hand in mine
and bring me home.
Thank you God for your love.
Thank you.

Amen.

Question for meditation:

Do I fully trust that with God at my side, I will find
my true home?

$\mathcal{H}$ENRI J. M. NOUWEN is the author of more than thirty books, among them: *Behold the Beauty of the Lord* and *Out of Solitude* (both published by Ave Maria Press). He has taught at the University of Notre Dame, Yale, and Harvard. Since 1986 he has been the pastor of L'Arche Daybreak in Toronto where he shares his life with people with mental disablilities.

$\mathcal{P}$HOTOGRAPHERS:

$\mathcal{J}$EAN-CLAUDE LEJEUNE was born in the suburbs of Paris, France. He has been working in the U.S. as a freelance photographer and a photography teacher since 1973. He describes his aim in this way: "to portray through photography what is human."

$\mathcal{G}$EORGE R. MERRILL, an Episcopal priest, resides in St. Michaels, Maryland. He is on the faculty of Loyola College in Maryland and serves as Clinical Pastoral Education Supervisor at Peninsula Regional Hospital in Salisbury, Maryland. His photographs appeared in *Refections: Psychological and Spiritual Images of the Heart*, a photo-meditation book, as well as in two other books and several periodicals.

$\mathcal{M}$ARIE ANTOINETTE PARISIO is a native of Brittany, France. She is currently a full-time homemaker in London, Ontario where she lives with her husband Tony and their three daughters. She has been associated with the L'Arche communities in Trosly-Breuil in France, in Palestine, and in Stratford and London in Canada.

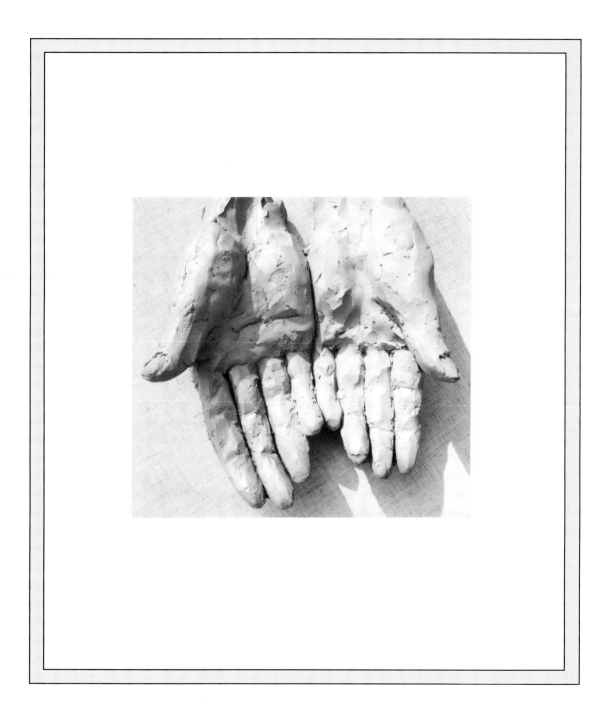